Put Beginning Readers on the Right Track with
ALL ABOARD READING™

The All Aboard Reading series is especially designed for beginning readers. Written by noted authors and illustrated in full color, these are books that children really want to read—books to excite their imagination, expand their interests, make them laugh, and support their feelings. With fiction and nonfiction stories that are high interest and curriculum-related, All Aboard Reading books offer something for every young reader. And with four different reading levels, the All Aboard Reading series lets you choose which books are most appropriate for your children and their growing abilities.

Picture Readers
Picture Readers have super-simple texts, with many nouns appearing as rebus pictures. At the end of each book are 24 flash cards—on one side is a rebus picture; on the other side is the written-out word.

Station Stop 1
Station Stop 1 books are best for children who have just begun to read. Simple words and big type make these early reading experiences more comfortable. Picture clues help children to figure out the words on the page. Lots of repetition throughout the text helps children to predict the next word or phrase—an essential step in developing word recognition.

Station Stop 2
Station Stop 2 books are written specifically for children who are reading with help. Short sentences make it easier for early readers to understand what they are reading. Simple plots and simple dialogue help children with reading comprehension.

Station Stop 3
Station Stop 3 books are perfect for children who are reading alone. With longer text and harder words, these books appeal to children who have mastered basic reading skills. More complex stories captivate children who are ready for more challenging books.

In addition to All Aboard Reading books, look for All Aboard Math Readers™ (fiction stories that teach math concepts children are learning in school); All Aboard Science Readers™ (nonfiction books that explore the most fascinating science topics in age-appropriate language); All Aboard Poetry Readers™ (funny, rhyming poems for readers of all levels); and All Aboard Mystery Readers™ (puzzling tales where children piece together evidence with the characters).

All Aboard for happy reading!

To Uncle Doug and Aunt Joyce—thank you for
the Christmases. And to Father Mark, an inspiration
throughout the year.—J.M.M.

For Harper—B.L.

ISBN: 978-0-545-22762-9

12 11 10 9 8 7 6 5 4 3 2 1   9 10 11 12 13 14/0

Printed in the U.S.A.   08

First Scholastic printing, December 2009

Illustrations by Bryan Langdo

No Room at the Inn
The Nativity Story

By Jean M. Malone
Illustrated by Bryan Langdo

SCHOLASTIC INC.
New York Toronto London Auckland
Sydney Mexico City New Delhi Hong Kong

Christmas is one of the most
wonderful times of the year.
Families come together to celebrate.
There are delicious meals, cookies,
and lots of presents!
But Christmas is about more
than meals, cookies, and presents.

Christmas is really the celebration
of a special birthday—
the birthday of Jesus Christ.

Jesus Christ was born
over 2,000 years ago.
Jesus's birthday is so important
because He is God's only Son.
He was born to bring peace to
the world.

We celebrate Christmas every year
to remember Jesus's very special birth.
The story of His birth is called
the Nativity (say: Nuh-TIV-uh-tee).

In the land of Galilee

(say: GAL-ill-ee),

there was a town called Nazareth

(say: Na-ZUH-reth).

A man named Joseph

lived in Nazareth.

Joseph was a carpenter.

He built things

like tables and benches.

Joseph planned to marry
a young woman named Mary.
He loved her very much.
Mary was a good woman.
She was sweet and kind.
Mary loved Joseph,
and she also loved God.

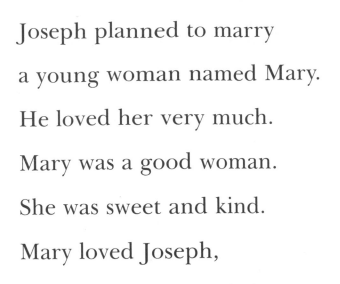

One day an angel came to visit Mary.

The angel was named Gabriel.

He was sent by God to ask Mary

an important request.

Gabriel asked Mary

to be the mother of God's Son.

Gabriel told Mary that

God's Son would be very special.

He would do great things.

He would help many people.

Mary was afraid.

But she was also very brave.

She trusted the Lord.

Mary told the angel
that she would do as God asked.
She would be the mother of the
Christ child.

Joseph was surprised when
Mary told him about her baby.
He did not know about God's plan.

Joseph was not sure whether
he was good enough to be
a father to such a special child.

That night, the angel Gabriel

came to see Joseph.

Gabriel told him not to worry.

Joseph would be a good father.

The baby would love him.

Gabriel told Joseph to name the child Jesus.

That year, the king wanted to know
how many people lived in the land.
To be counted, Joseph and Mary
needed to go to Bethlehem
in Judea (say: Joo-DAY-uh).

MEDITERRANEAN
SEA

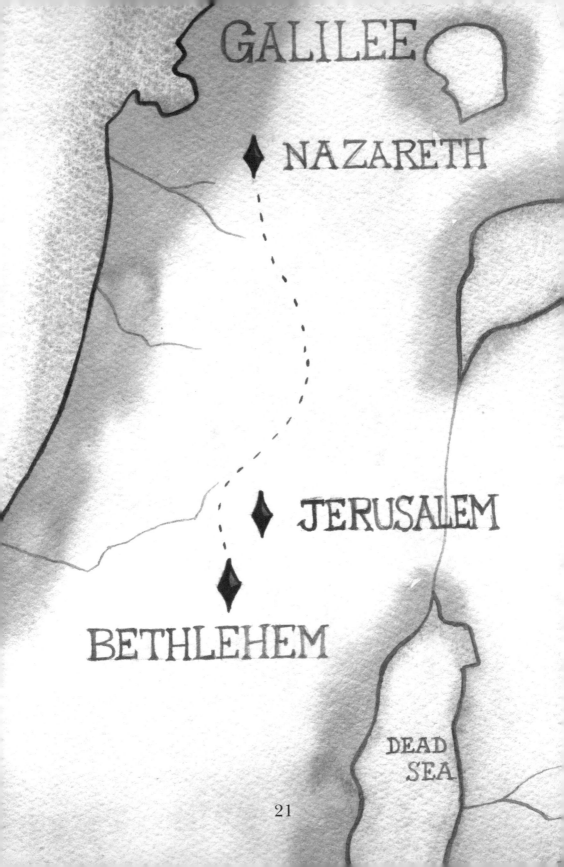

GALILEE

NAZARETH

JERUSALEM

BETHLEHEM

DEAD
SEA

It was a very long journey to Bethlehem.

Joseph walked the whole way.

It was almost time

for Mary to have her baby.

She was too big to walk,

so she rode an old, brown donkey

to Bethlehem.

It was late at night when Mary

and Joseph reached Bethlehem.

They were tired and hungry.

But there was no room at any of the inns.

One innkeeper wanted to

help the young couple.

He said they could stay in his stable.

It was full of animals, but it was warm.

Mary and Joseph were very thankful

to have a place to rest.

That night in the stable,

Mary gave birth to Jesus Christ,

the Son of God.

Mary didn't have clothes
or a cradle for her baby.
She wrapped Him in strips of cloth
called swaddling clothes.
She laid Him in the manger as a bed.
Mangers are racks that hold hay
for animals to eat.

The animals didn't mind sharing
their stable or their manger.
They knew that baby Jesus was special.

When Jesus was born,

a big, bright star rose in the sky.

The star was right over the stable

to tell the whole world

that this amazing baby

had been born that night.

In lands far away in the East,

three wise men called Magi

(say: MAJ-eye)

studied the stars.

They saw the star of Bethlehem.

They knew it meant that

a great king had been born.

So the Magi set off on a journey.

They wanted to find the king

and His star.

In the fields outside Bethlehem,
shepherds guarded their sheep
from wolves and thieves.
They saw the new star, too.
They wondered what it meant.

The angel Gabriel
came to the shepherds.
He told them that he had good news.
The shepherds had never seen
an angel before.
They were afraid.
But Gabriel told the shepherds
that they had nothing to fear.

He explained that Jesus
had just been born,
and He would
bring peace to the world.
The shepherds should rejoice!
Then he told them where
to find the newborn baby.

Suddenly, a choir of angels
appeared in the sky.
The angels sang, "Glory to God,"
and, "Peace on earth, good will to men."

The shepherds were not scared anymore.

They went straight into Bethlehem.

They found the stable under the star.

The shepherds knelt before baby Jesus.

He was still asleep in His manger bed.

They rejoiced because Jesus had been born.

They told everyone they knew

about the special baby.

Later, the Magi from the East
found the stable, too.
They knelt before Jesus
with gifts they had brought for Him.

One of the wise men

brought a gift of gold.

The second wise man
brought frankincense
(say: FRANK-in-sense),
a kind of candle.

The last wise man brought myrrh
(say: mer).

Myrrh is a sweet-smelling oil.

The wise men brought gifts to Jesus
to show their respect and honor.
They knew that He would be a
very great man.
Today we give presents
in honor of Jesus's birthday.

People remember the story
of the Nativity in many ways.
Some people light candles.
Other people sing carols.

Many people put stars or angels
on their Christmas trees.

It is important to remember

Jesus's birthday at Christmas.

Because He was a special baby.

And Christmas is a special day.